Several years ago I heard the Lord _____ ___ _p. I said "How Lord?" He said "I will show you." Since that _____ ___ ___s allowed me to have a flock of prayer warriors that show up faithfully to pray for the school and another flock that intercedes on behalf of the church youth.

In putting this book together Amelia Weaver was invaluable in editing and formatting. I am so thankful for Tom Temple's expertise on the cover. Deana Bass has encouraged me as a cheerleader believing this devotional was a project worth completing. Heather Young helped me set up my blog.

I am so thankful for my army of prayer warriors that have been my Aaron and Hur on the journey of life. I would not want to do life without you. I also am so blessed by my family whom I love with all of my heart.

Dedicated to those who have allowed me to walk with them through the crucible of suffering: Frances, my Mom, Patty, Irna, Monica, Jane, the Clarks, Debbi, and my small group.

Blog: https://extraordinaryintheordinaryblog.wordpress.com

Email: extraordinaryintheordinaryblog@gmail.com

The photo on the front cover I took in my front yard as a beautiful butterfly with a broken wing was on my flowers. It represents to me God's love for me in the details of the beautiful in the brokenness of life. The back cover photo is a ladybug that was on my front door the day I finished this book. God always shows up miraculously and extraordinarily in the ordinary of life.

All scripture references are from the New International Version unless otherwise noted.

About Me

At 9, I realized that my faith had to be my own, that there was not a family plan for the gospel like insurance or cell phones. I asked Jesus into my heart and began a great adventure.

I am an educator, a storyteller, a mom, who loves prayer and people. I heard a speaker, Dawn Neely, say prayer began as desperation, became a discipline, and now is her passion. That is my story as well.

I have been running hard after the Lord all these years and He has shown up beyond what I can imagine.

When Mom was dying in 2011, I saw Him show up in every detail. He carried me through something I had dreaded my whole life. I realized I could trust Him with the rest of my life.

I found what I read in *Hudson Taylor's Spiritual Secret* referred to as the **great exchange** – exchanging my wants, needs, desires, and life for His – to be true. Since my great exchange, God reminds me daily of His great love for me. One of those ways is through nature. With yellow butterflies by my front door and ladybugs on my windshield, He freaks me out with His scandalous love for me when I least expect.

He is transcendent – infinite and huge, yet eminent – close and dear. The more I look for Him, the more I see Him. The more I surrender to Him, the more He gives me peace and direction. As I rest in Him and wait on Him, I see Him able to use me more to further His kingdom. He shows me constantly extraordinary in the ordinary.

I'm excited for you to see it too!
Love you!
Lanie

CONTENTS

Ladybugs And Yellow Butterflies

It is fun to pick something in nature and when you see it, you are reminded of the Lord's great love for you. *For since the creation of the world God's invisible qualities – His eternal power and divine nature – have been clearly seen, being understood from what has been made, so that men are without excuse.* Romans 1:20

I chose ladybugs and yellow butterflies.

One day I walked into my bathroom and there was this ladybug on my mirror. "Jesus loves me!"

He loves you too and longs to show you. *Yet the Lord longs to be gracious to you; therefore He will rise up to show you compassion. For the Lord is a God of justice. Blessed are all who wait for Him!* Isaiah 30:18

Pray about it and choose something in nature for the Lord to remind you of His great love for you.

Now watch for it! Look for Him to show up and reveal His love for you. God is not a god in hiding.

You will seek me and find me when you seek me with all your heart. Jeremiah 29:13

On my recent birthday, I was driving along and right in my line of vision on the inside of my windshield was a ladybug. Wow! Happy Birthday to me from Jesus! God rocks!

Scripture:

You have searched me, Lord and you know me. You know when I set and when I rise; you perceive my thoughts from afar. You discern my going out and my lying down; you are familiar with all my ways. Before a word is on my tongue you, Lord, know it completely. You hem me in behind and before, and you lay your hand upon me. Psalm 139:1-5

What Do We Pore Over

I had a dear friend with breast cancer and I was always amazed during my visits with her as she went through surgery, treatments and recovery that I could so clearly see Jesus in her. Every visit felt like a personal encounter with Christ, (*Christ in her the hope of glory*. Colossians 1:27) When I asked her about it she shared with me that every day she would pore over the Psalms and daily used Ruth Meyer's book *31 Days of Praise* which compiles various scripture into praises. She typed up all of the scriptures used and shared them with me.

Years ago I heard a guest pastor say that when he was growing up his mom would pore over this book every morning and pore over it in the evening and if she got time in the afternoon she would spend some time in it. I was expecting him to say the Bible, but it was the Sears catalog. That illustration has really stuck with me through the years. What am I poring over? If I have a few minutes, what do I run to? Is it social media, or a game on my phone or NPR or the news? What is the result in my life of poring over things other than the word of God?

Now with smart phones and Bible apps we can even have scripture read to us. I love it when I have an athlete at work with a religion class and they get so excited about the Bible app that can read their assignment to them. Am I that excited about hearing and reading the word of God which is so powerful that it can work change in my heart and life?

Scripture:

How blessed is the man who does not walk in the counsel of the wicked. Nor stand in the path of sinners, nor sit in the seat of scoffers! But his delight is in the law of the LORD. And in His law he meditates day and night. He will be like a tree firmly planted by streams of water. Which yields its fruit in its season and its leaf does not wither; and in whatever he does, he prospers. Psalm 1:1-3

Let my meditation be pleasing to Him; As for me, I shall be glad in the LORD. Psalm 104:34

Failure To Notice

I love it any time my kids come home. It is always interesting when they have been away for a while and come in, the things they notice. It usually brings to light the things I daily fail to notice.

We were loading the dishwasher and one asked why I randomly put in the glasses instead of going from front to back. Wow! It had not occurred to me. It was an easy adjustment and made much more sense.

Next they realized that many of the glasses came out with spots. I would just rewash them. (I know…brilliant!) One said, why are you doing the same thing over and over again if it is not working. Duh? It had not occurred to me either. I switched the cycle and added a rinse agent and voila! Amazing how much time is being saved not rewashing glasses. I have heard insanity is doing the same thing over and over expecting different results.

I was at a wedding recently and there was a Navy Seal there who used the words "situational awareness." I had never heard that military term but I love it. Am I "situationally aware"?

Just like I was failing to notice obvious inefficient habits, it is easy to fail to notice things in our lives that with some conviction and awareness could be life changing. I have found the best way to identify these things that I fail to notice is by being a part of a community that I can trust and that I have invited to speak truth into my life. I can go to them with situations in my life and allow them to give me perspective and objectivity. When I am in the situation, I am too close to it to see the big picture.

One area where I have especially needed this in my life is when there are emotional situations involving my children. I have realized that happens especially in situations where one of my children might have been wronged. I get emotional, lose my objectivity and sin. I have learned to try to remember to pray first about the situation and the people involved and then to seek wise counsel before responding.

Scripture:

My dear brothers and sisters, take note of this: Everyone should be quick to listen, slow to speak and slow to become angry. James 1:19 NIV

Do not forsake wisdom, and she will protect you; love her, and she will watch over you. The beginning of wisdom is this: Get wisdom. Though it cost all you have, get understanding. Proverbs 4:6-7

Obedience Brings Blessing

When I was in college I was running hard after Jesus, in two fellowship groups, two Bible studies and in two accountability relationships. But I did not really like myself. Outwardly I was joyful, but inwardly I was insecure.

I started dating a guy I met in one of the fellowship groups. He had done more than he wanted in a previous relationship and decided at the outset that our relationship would be holy. We dated a year and did not kiss. The song "Your Kiss is on my List" came out while we were dating and was very appropriate. The amazing thing though was that by his wanting a relationship with me without wanting anything from me physically totally transformed me from within. I realized that if here was a guy who loved me for who I was, and not what I could give him, how much more did Jesus love me as I was and not as I should be.

His obedience brought great blessing to my life and still today one of my favorite gifts from Jesus (a gift mainly from this relationship) is that I like myself. When you like yourself, you are able to take risks and reach out to others.

Also, because we did not spend time in the physical, we spent hours communicating. I learned so much about him and myself. I had gone to visit his family for a wedding when my father died in a plane crash. Our relationship was starting to fizzle, but I still had feelings for him. I went back to school the day of my dad's funeral and prayed that if the relationship was not from the Lord that He would remove my feelings for this guy. Within 24 hours, the Lord totally changed my heart. I was not even attracted to him anymore. It was such a blessing. God knew what I could handle. Since we had not been physical, we were able to continue our friendship. I became friends with the girl he began dating and ended up being in their wedding. God's ways are much higher than our ways.

Obedience brings blessing. Disobedience brings disaster. The ripple effect of one person's obedience is deep and wide. I learned so much from that relationship. When I am surrendering my heart and life to the Lord, He can channel my heart wherever He pleases. I learned that I could totally trust God with my heart. When I do it His way, the blessings are huge. He is in all of the details and does not waste anything. His laws are for our protection, not to punish us. He is about life and love and freedom and intimacy.

Scripture:

The thief comes only to steal and kill and destroy; I have come that they may have life, and have it to the full.
John 10:10

And this is love: that we walk in obedience to his commands. As you have heard from the beginning, his command is that you walk in love. 2 John 1:6

Blessed Suffering

Blessed suffering – seems like a contradiction in terms.

At the end of my sweet friend Irna's life, I was staying with her one night and she was coughing so hard. It was unbearable. I was standing beside her bed crying out to God to stop it and asking Him why she was having to suffer so. She raised her hand forcefully in praise to Him in the midst of her suffering and I started singing the doxology, "Praise God from whom all blessings flow." In the midst of the suffering there was worship.

She had early on told me that one of her prayers was that she could have the faith of Shadrach, Meshach and Abednego. That even if the Lord did not save her, that her faith would be strong. In that moment, I knew that her prayer had been answered.

We had many heart wrenching discussions but especially in her last two weeks about being "ready." She had asked me to help her process and "get ready." In the midst of that coughing she reached a point where she was ready to let go. I saw that God used her suffering to help her let go of this world and prepare her for the next.

I think of Paul who suffered so much. There were times when he could have died, but the Lord intervened. Paul should have died when he got bitten by a viper. He should not have survived a huge storm and being shipwrecked, but the Lord saved him as well as all those with him. It helps me to see suffering in a different light. I believe God uses our struggles at times to wrench us away from this world and allow us a more eternal perspective.

Scripture:

For our light and momentary troubles are achieving for us an eternal glory that far outweighs them all. So that we fix our eyes not on what is seen, but on what is unseen, since what is seen is temporary, but what is unseen is eternal. 2 Corinthians 4:17-18

But our citizenship is in heaven. And we eagerly await at Savior from there, the Lord Jesus Christ. Philippians 3:20 NIV

Kindness

When I was in middle school one of my "friends" would decide each day who was "in" and who was "out". I knew that deep down it did not feel right but I did not have my "sea legs" to stand up against it. One day though it was my turn to be out. It was the worst. It was a life lesson though for me that there is never a reason to be unkind. It was life changing. It helps me even now to see how the Lord used that difficult relational lesson to make me aware of the bigger picture and the importance of kindness. I often see Christians being unkind to one another or not supporting each other. I think, seriously? We are on the same team.

I heard on the radio that you don't have to see eye to eye to walk hand in hand. I think Satan uses petty squabbles to prevent us from working together to solve poverty and world hunger. If every believer surrendered their own agenda and just rested in the Lord and His leading we would be making kingdom impact that would make nonbelievers unable to deny the existence of Christ. A friend was saying that her daughter who is critical of Christians cares about poverty but is not doing anything about it. If she saw first hand the Christian community taking care of the poor and sick and downtrodden it would change her impression of Christianity.

Gandhi said "I like their Christ, but I don't like their Christian." Dietrich Bonhoeffer said that your life as a Christian should make non-Christians question their disbelief in Christ.

I want Christ to be so real in my life that others see Him when they look at me, like Moses where His glow was so great, he had to wear a veil to keep from blinding the Israelites.

Scripture:

Therefore, I urge you, brothers and sisters, in view of God's mercy, to offer your bodies as a living sacrifice, holy and pleasing to God – this is your true and proper worship. Romans 12:1, 2

Dear children, let us not love with words or speech, but with actions and in truth. 1 John 3:18

Dear friends, let us love one another; for love comes from God. Everyone who loves has been born of God and knows God. 1 John 4:7

Do You Know Their Name?

On the way home from church one Sunday, I stopped by to get bagels for my family. I was on the phone with someone as I pulled into a parking space. A woman came up to the car and asked if I would buy a keychain she had made. Fear came up from within me. I am ashamed to say I did not look her in the eye, did not buy a keychain and finished my phone conversation.

While getting my bagels the Lord really convicted me. When I came back out I pulled a gift card out of my wallet to give to her. I searched the parking lot and she was gone. I had missed my chance. I prayed for her.

I tutored a religion class on introduction to the Bible. I was amazed at how important social justice was to the Lord. The Lord has such a heart for the poor, oppressed and downtrodden and desires for us to have a heart for them as well. He calls us to care for them. If we are oppressed in a situation, he is for us. He hates oppression of any kind. Nothing about the Lord is oppressive.

The Lord gave me a second chance and an opportunity to help with the local prison ministry by doing songs, stories and crafts with the children of prisoners during their Sunday afternoon visitation. I was so blessed. The children were precious and their parents so appreciative. I think I had this image of the poor and the imprisoned, but they are just people like me. I could easily be in their same situation. Kelly Minter in a Bible study asked if we knew a poor person's name. That question really brought my lack of engagement outside of my comfortable life home to me. When you have a name that connects you to a life you are bridging a gap and allowing the Lord to impact both of you.

Scripture:

Truly I tell you, whatever you did for one of the least of these brothers and sisters of mine, you did for me. Matthew 25:40

Give justice to the weak and fatherless; maintain the right of the afflicted and the destitute. Rescue the weak and the needy; deliver them from the hand of the wicked. Psalm 82:3-4

She opens her hand to the poor and reaches out her hands to the needy. Proverbs 31:20

Sons And Daughters

I went to the memorial service for a friend's mom who became my friend. Her passing was a huge loss to me because every time I saw her I always felt like I was so special and loved. When I saw her, her face would light up; she was always so excited to see me. After her service each person I talked to said the same thing. They each had felt so loved by her. Her love for the others in no way diminished her love for me. We were all her "adopted" daughters.

We are adopted sons and daughters of the King. I think a lot of times we feel like "step" children. We are like Cinderella sitting in the corner with our broom covered in ashes bemoaning the many tasks at hand instead of relishing in our prince and princess status. We, because of Christ, are the children of the king, not with entitlement of our status, but servant leaders privileged to be the hands and feet of the king in his kingdom.

A good friend at work loves to hear my God stories. She said recently that there is me and then there is every one else, implying that He loves me more than everyone else. I told her that yes, Jesus loves me, but it is a bold face lie that He loves me more than her. It is a lie that He loves me more than YOU! Jesus loves you! Let me say it again JESUS LOVES YOU! He loves you as you are, not as you should be. *He longs to be gracious to you. He rises to show you compassion.* (Isaiah 30:18) *He rejoices over you with singing. He quiets you with His love.* (Zephaniah 3:17) *You are precious and honored in His sight and He loves you!* (Isaiah 43:4)

When my children were growing up after dinner a lot of nights we would play "love tank". I would pull my chair back and say who needs to fill up their love tank and anyone that wanted to could sit in my lap for as long as they wanted or until someone pushed them out. Jesus wants you to crawl into His lap. Corrie Ten Boom said "Nestle, don't wrestle". He wants to hold you close, while you pour your heart out to Him.

Scripture:

For I am persuaded, that neither death, nor life, nor angels, nor principalities, nor things present, nor things to come, nor powers, nor height, nor depth, nor any other creature, shall be able to separate us from the love of God, which is in Christ Jesus our Lord. Romans 8:38-39

She gave this name to the Lord who spoke to her: 'You are the God who sees me,' for she said, 'I have now seen the One who sees me.' Genesis 16:13

No Downside To Being Loving

I was listening to Focus on the Family on my way home from work one night and the woman being interviewed said "There is no downside to being loving." I thought "Yes!" and as soon as I got home typed it into my phone to make sure I remembered that line to use some time, of course assuming I would be on the receiving end.

The very next morning I was getting ready to walk out the door to work, I had my lunch, bag and computer all packed and ready to go when that line came back to me -"There is no downside to being loving." I had assumed that I would be on the receiving end, but the Lord was speaking to me as the giver.

My husband had come down earlier complaining that his back hurt and was in the living room watching TV. At that moment I had to decide in a split second if I was going to obey or not. I begrudgingly set down all of my stuff and walked into the living room, and asked him if he would like for me to rub his back. He said yes. I prayed for him as I rubbed his back.

I saw almost immediately the blessing of obedience. I was energized to surrender completely to the Lord, knowing once again that He is in the details and that I can trust Him completely.

Scripture:

I have been crucified with Christ and I no longer live, but Christ lives in me. The life I live in the body, I live by faith in the Son of God, who loved me and gave himself for me. Galatians 2:20

And so we know and rely on the love God has for us. God is love. Whoever lives in love lives in God, and God in him. 1 John 4:16

We love because He first loved us. If anyone says, 'I love God,' yet hates his brother, he is liar. For anyone who does not love his brother, whom he has seen, cannot love God, whom he has not seen. 1 John 4:19-20

Sweet Conviction

The first week of school, I was driving to my husband's office to go together to my son's soccer game and was unaware that I was going through a school zone. A motorcycle policeman came out of the bushes and pulled me over. My 30 plus year record for not having a speeding ticket was broken. Huge bummer! I can come up with a lot of excuses, but bottom line, I broke the law and there were consequences, very expensive consequences.

I tutored an Introduction to the Bible class last semester and one of the themes was that we can be unintentionally unclean, but we have to be intentionally holy. That resonated with me. I mess up all of the time, often it is unintentional. I did not realize I was speeding. Even though I was not trying to mess up, there were still consequences and I still missed the mark. Jesus died for all of our mess ups, the blatant ones as well as the unintentional. His grace covers it all. It is important to pray for conviction and to pray for truth.

We may be unintentionally unclean, but holiness comes from being intentional. Holiness does not just happen. We don't fall into being holy. We need to pray about our decisions: what we watch, what we hear, how we spend our time. Every day we make decisions that can draw us near to the Lord or separate us from Him. It is a relationship like any other. If there is no investment in that relationship then the relationship will not develop.

Holiness is a natural outpouring of our relationship with Him and His loving conviction. When we take a baby step toward God, He takes a Father leap toward us. I love that about Him! He has shown us how much He desires a relationship with us by sacrificing Christ. He is not a God in hiding. He knows us and wants to be known by us. When we are praying for conviction, he will show us and when we repent we draw near to Him.

Pray to feel the sweet conviction of the Lord, knowing that conviction draws us in deeper in our relationship with the Lord and that there is no condemnation in Christ.

Scripture:

Therefore, there is now no condemnation for those who are in Christ Jesus because through Christ Jesus the law of the Spirit who gives life has set you free from the law of sin and death. Romans 8:1, 2

□□□□□□□□□□□□□□□□□□□□□□□□□□□□*If my people, who are called by my name, will humble themselves and pray and seek my face and turn from their wicked ways, then I will hear from heaven, and I will forgive their sin and will heal their land*□□□□□□□□. 2 Chronicles□ 7:14□□□□□□□□□□□□□

If we confess our sin, He is faithful and just and will cleanse us from all unrighteousness. 1 John 1:9

Giving Thanks In All Circumstances

My sophomore year at UNC, I broke my leg. I was on crutches for several weeks and then in a cast almost the whole semester. 1 Thessalonians 5:16-18 *Rejoice always, pray continually, give thanks in all circumstances; for this is God's will for you in Christ Jesus.* was my theme verse during that time.

I remember one day I was on crutches and it had snowed. I had my cast in a plastic bag and my backpack on my back. I felt and looked ridiculous. You know that feeling when you are just weary to the bones. I just wanted to sit down on the pavement and cry. I was so done and that verse came to me. I stopped and quoted it, breaking it down in my head, going through and 1) rejoicing, 2) praying for what I needed and 3) giving thanks in my circumstances and surrendering to the Lord.

The Lord met me in my dark place and gave me what I needed to keep going. I remember experiencing inexpressible joy bubbling up from somewhere deep within me that I knew was coming from the Lord. The joy was not tied at all to my circumstances.

When the Lord is in us, the word of God is alive and active. (Hebrews 4:12) It is important to be in the word and memorizing the word so that the Lord can bring it to our minds and hearts at the moment we need it, so that we can correctly handle the word of truth. (2 Timothy 2:15)

As I look back, that season of what seemed really hard at the time, prepared me for future seasons that were even harder. It was a sweet time of leaning into the Lord and Him showing up in the details. When I hear that verse, it is an "ebenezer" reminding me of God's faithfulness. It also reminds me how He used that verse to help me and of the power of being in the word and rejoicing, praying, and especially thanking the Lord.

Please pray to see the word of God come alive.

Scripture:

The Lord is close to the brokenhearted and saves those who are crushed in spirit. Psalm 34:18

Rejoice always, pray continually, give thanks in all circumstances; for this is God's will for you in Christ Jesus. 1 Thessalonians 5:16-18

For the word of God is alive and active. Sharper than any double-edged sword, it penetrates even to dividing soul and spirit, joints and marrow; it judges the thoughts and attitudes of the heart. Hebrews 4:12

Do your best to present yourself to God as one approved, a worker who does not need to be ashamed and who correctly handles the word of truth. 2 Timothy 2:15

A Donkey to Ride On

Gary Chapman quoted his son Derek as saying "sometimes the Lord just needs a donkey to ride on." I think of that often.

That semester I broke my leg, I was taking a religion class. I had a recitation on Fridays on the third floor of a building with no elevator. You can imagine how the thought of climbing those stairs with my backpack and crutches was so discouraging. I had a friend who would meet me there and literally carry me and my books up those flights of stairs. I remember one time after carrying me up the stairs he didn't even stay for the recitation. I couldn't believe he had gotten out of bed and walked over just to help me make my class.

John Piper said "Do you feel more loved by God when He makes much of you or when you make much of Him?" For me it is definitely when He allows me to make much of Him.

Pray for eyes to see God show up in your life as well as specific ways to show up in the lives of others.

Learn the blessing of showing up for others which builds community.

Scripture:

Give and it will be given to you. A good measure, pressed down, shaken together and running over, will be poured into your lap. For with the measure you use, it will be measured to you. Luke 6:38

Cast all your cares upon Him because He cares for you. 1 Peter 5:7

Numb Or Feel

I have had friends and family that have had surgery and/or cancer that have had to go on narcotics for the pain. The narcotics work great to numb the pain, but they shut down the GI system. If you have ever had this happen to you, from what I can tell, it is absolutely miserable. Becoming impacted and things not working properly makes one feel awful. I have prayed fervently in these situations for bowels to move.

 I think with the pain of life many times we use our own "narcotics" to numb the pain: shopping, alcohol, drugs, stuffing it, or just putting on a happy face. When we numb the pain, things get stopped up. It may not be today, or tomorrow or next week, but at some point we realize we are miserable. Things are not working properly. Functions that should be natural do not come naturally. We are not even sure why or how we got there. Just like the GI issues, it takes extreme measures at that point to get things moving again and those extreme measures have their own side effects. At that point though, our options are limited.

All of this to say, it is much more beneficial to daily work on the pain, processing and allowing God to bring light to the darkness. We must lean into Him and allow Him to enter into our misery, to work out our salvation daily with fear and trembling. It is important to have community we can go to and process our struggles inviting them to walk with us through the hard of life and to speak truth into our situation. I find that shame and pride are two things that tend to prevent me from sharing the hard of my story with others. As I am learning to do this I am amazed at how when I share, others bless me and my story blesses them. I am also so encouraged because I have others praying for me and sharing my burdens. Sometimes just merely telling someone brings light to the darkness. I am amazed at how much lighter I feel after sharing with others and especially feeling the blessing and power of their prayers. Sharing on a regular basis allows all functions to run more efficiently the majority of the time.

Scripture:

Do not grieve like the rest of mankind, who have no hope. 1 Thessalonians 4:13

Cast your bread upon the waters, for you will find it after many days. Ecclesiastes 11:1

Carry each other's burdens, and in this way you will fulfill the law of Christ. Galatians 6:2

Pride Versus Humility

One of my biggest struggles is with pride. It is a constant battle.

I would love to be humble instead of prideful, but it is something that comes from within. I can't just say I want to be humble and I don't want to be prideful. It is intimacy with Christ that produces humility. It flows out of our relationship with Christ.

There are so many Bible verses warning about pride. The Lord convicts me often of pride. It is not until after I say something or think something that I am convicted that I am prideful. I have this internal battle where God will allow me to be a part of something great that He does. I think "God rocks!" Quickly, though, it turns to "I rock!" He convicts me and I repent and go back to "God rocks". It goes round and round. I am so thankful though for the conviction, because it reminds me that He loves me and cares and wants to help me be more like Him.

Humility and authenticity draw people in and pride pushes people away. I believe it all goes back to just running hard after Jesus and allowing Him to transform us from within. The more we get to know Him, the more we want to know Him, and the more He helps us be more like Him and helps us understand ourselves. It's a beautiful thing.

Pray for an internal transforming work of the Holy Spirit and to not be conformed to this world, but be transformed by the renewing your mind.

Scripture:

My son, do not despise the Lord's discipline, and do not resent his rebuke, because the lord disciplines those He loves, as a father the son he delights in. Proverbs 3:11

Therefore, I urge you brothers and sisters, in view of God's mercy, to offer your bodies as a living sacrifice, holy and pleasing to God - this is your true and proper worship. Do not conform to the pattern of this world, but be transformed by the renewing of your mind. Then you will be able to test and approve what God's will is -His good, pleasing and perfect will. Romans 12:1, 2

Perspective

I used to hate rainy days, but then my children gave me a really fun pair of rain boots for my birthday. Now I love rainy days because I get to wear my fun rain boots that remind me of my precious children whom I dearly love.

It is amazing how one little thing can change our whole perspective. It is so important to pray for truth and also to allow others to speak truth into our lives. Leslie Vernick said that if you are the only voice you are listening to, you are in a very dark place.

I have been reading about Joseph in my quiet time. He had years in dark places. He was betrayed by his brothers, falsely accused by his employer, forgotten by his cell mate, but when he had a chance to seek revenge what was his response? *Do not be distressed and do not be angry with yourselves for selling me here, because it was to save lives that God sent me ahead of you.* Genesis 45:5 Wow, that is a different perspective. Joseph's perspective could have only come from the Lord.

Many are in very dark places. Please pray that the light of Christ will take away the darkness. Pray to hear truth and receive it. Seek out people in your life and invite them to speak truth to you.

Scripture:

In Him was life, and that life was the light of all mankind. The light shines in the darkness, and the darkness has not overcome it. John 1:5

But love your enemies, do good to them ... Then your reward will be great, and you will be children of the Most High, because he is kind to the ungrateful and wicked. Be merciful, just as your Father is merciful. Luke 6:35-36

Is God Still God?

What happens when the worst thing that can happen happens? Is God still God? Is He still enough? Will we still trust Him? I had a friend who had two children that were really sick. She talked to another mom who had a son with a brain tumor. She said to her, you have to go to the worst place and decide, if both of your children die will God still be God? Will He still be enough? Can you still trust Him? Her children both passed away three months apart. Her worst nightmare occurred and she found the Lord to be a solid rock she could stand on.

I think of that often and when I start worrying about something, I take myself there. If my worst case scenario becomes my reality, will that change who God is in my life and will He walk me through the hard? Many times I do not understand, but I trust Him. Just yesterday I heard of several huge losses of dear lives. I do not begin to understand. Many who have traumatic losses and events blame God. When that happens they cut off the very source of their help and healing. The Lord is about bringing beauty from ashes. He wastes nothing that we go through. He is about healing the brokenhearted. He is present in our hard. Run to Him, He will catch you and lift you up. He takes what Satan means for evil in our lives and redeems it.

As you walk through hard things in your life run to Jesus and allow Him to meet you in your pit and give you a firm place to stand.

Scripture:

I waited patiently for the Lord; he turned to me and heard my cry. He lifted me out of the slimy pit, out of the mud and mire; he set my feet on a rock and gave me a firm place to stand. He put a new song in my mouth, a hymn of praise to our God. Many will see and fear the Lord and put their trust in Him. Psalm 40:1-3

The Lord is close to the broken hearted and saves those who are crushed in spirit. Psalm 34:18

Stories

We all have a story. No one can argue with your story. Paul shared the gospel by sharing his story. His was really exciting. In Acts 22:6-8 *About noon as I came near Damascus, suddenly a bright light from heaven flashed around me. I fell to the ground and heard a voice say to me, 'Saul! Saul! Why do you persecute me?' 'Who are you Lord'? I asked.*

You can continue reading the story, but you get the picture. Paul was one of the greatest missionaries ever and his technique was just to tell his story--where and how he encountered Jesus and the impact it had on his life.

I started going to church when I was barely out of the womb. When I was 9, I realized that it was not a family plan, like insurance or a cell phone. I needed to ask Jesus into my heart. I did and was baptized. When I was in middle school the whole friend thing was not going so well and I realized that He was my best friend and other friends were coming and going but *he is the friend that sticks closer than a brother* (Proverbs 18:24) and *greater love has no one than this, to lay down one's life for one's friend.* John 15:13

When I was in college and my dad died in a plane crash, I realized that God was my daddy, my Abba, my Jehovah Jireh, my provider, my Jehovah Rapha, my healer, my tower of refuge and strength. (Matthew 7:9-11)

When I was single, I realized that God was my husband, my beloved, my kinsman redeemer and the lover of my soul. *Your maker is your husband.* (Isaiah 54:5)

It was in the hardness of life, that I found the Lord showing up as my best friend, my daddy and my husband. The Lord found me. He is called the hound of heaven. How did he find you? What is your story?

Pray to encounter the Lord as your best friend, daddy, kinsmen redeemer and lover of your soul.

Scripture:

The Lord your God is in your midst, the Mighty One, will save. He will rejoice over you with gladness, He will quiet you with His love, He will rejoice over you with singing. Zephaniah 3:17 NKJV

The thief comes only to steal and kill and destroy; I have come that they may have life, and have it to the full. John 10:10

Wisdom

There are several things that I pray regularly for my children and one of them is wisdom. On my younger son's 18th birthday, I asked men in his life to send him words of wisdom as he heads into adulthood. Below is what his older brother sent him and I was so encouraged seeing tangible evidence of the Lord answering my prayers for wisdom.

Here are a few words of wisdom that I try to live by and I think you should too.

Perspective is reality. The amount of enjoyment you get out of any particular situation is up to you. Choose to see the glass as half full and have some fun. When the glass seems completely empty, laugh. Life is much more fun when you laugh.

3 Year Rule. Learn to distinguish short-term problems from long-term problems and react accordingly. Life is going to throw some challenges and obstacles your way - some big, but mostly small. If the problem you are faced with won't matter in 3 years, don't make a big deal of it. Do what needs to be done to fix the issue and move on.

Communication matters. Most problems can be solved before they start with good communication.

Be kind. There is no reason not to be kind to others, and it makes life a lot easier. However, the squeaky wheel gets the grease. The be-kind rule does not apply to cable companies and the like.

Find failure. You really can do just about anything you set your mind to, but it almost always involves working harder than anyone else and enduring many failures along the way. Don't be afraid to fail. A failure just means you set your goal appropriately high. And after you fail, don't be afraid to work harder than anyone else to ensure that your failure is a jumping board for future success.

Finally, learn to give. Giving is more rewarding than receiving. Give often and don't expect anything in return.

Scripture:

For wisdom is more precious than rubies, and nothing you desire can compare with her. Proverbs 8:11

If any of you lacks wisdom, you should ask God, who gives generously to all without finding fault, and it will be given to you. James 1:5

Walk by the Spirit

On my mom's side of the family we have a week long family reunion every 3rd year since I was 6. She was one of 7 and the only one that lived east of the Mississippi. I am thankful to know my cousins and their children from all over the US. One cousin's son asked me at one of the reunions to pray for purity which was an area in which he was struggling. I have been praying for a few years and occasionally check in to ask how he is doing and to remind him of my prayers. I got this message from him recently.

> "I just wanted to let you know that I have been blessed with such victory over impurity in my life really since the beginning of last October, in ways that I cannot describe other than a miraculous work of the Spirit. All praise to God. I so much appreciate your prayer and care for me, and I wanted to let you know what God has been doing in my life."

This is an area where Satan knows he can do much damage against the kingdom. He is a liar. The world is bombarding us with His lies at every opportunity. Satan knows where we are vulnerable.

You hear constantly of Christian leaders taking a fall in this area. Obedience brings blessing and disobedience brings disaster to the whole community. If we don't think it will happen to us, then we are especially vulnerable. In areas where we struggle, it is important to intentionally pray specifically and also to share with someone who will pray and be willing to hold us accountable. The Lord brings light to the darkness. Satan wants to take us down, shame and isolate us. We need to be on our guard against his schemes. We need to be careful not to put ourselves in risky situations. I always liked the phrase "stay public and vertical". We need to make wise choices. If we get in a situation where we feel uncomfortable, we need to immediately flee and/or call someone. God promises when we are tempted to provide a way out. 1 Cor 10:13

What did my cousin's son do right? He admitted it was a struggle, shared with someone that he was struggling, asked for prayer and accountability, and continued to run hard after Jesus. He gained victory in Christ, which was only explainable by the working of God in his life. It encouraged him for future struggles. It encouraged me. What a privilege to share in others' victory as part of community.

Please pray to see the blessing of obedience and purity and the need for community and accountability.

Scripture:

So I say, walk by the Spirit, and you will not gratify the desires of the flesh. For the flesh desires what is contrary to the Spirit, and the Spirit what is contrary to the flesh. They are in conflict with each other, so that you are not to do whatever you want. Galatians 5:16-17

Strong Woman, Soft Heart

My mom was a strong woman with a soft heart. Instead of the hard in her life making her hardhearted, the Lord used the hard in her life to make her compassionate. Her mom died of cancer when she was 21, her dad died of a heart attack when she was 36, her husband was killed in a plane crash at 49 and left her a widow with 4 children running a family business on her own. Instead of blaming God, she leaned into Him and He was her passion and life. As a result, He made her a strong woman with a soft heart. She could minister to others with compassion and gentleness because she had known the ministry of Christ in her own hard
.

Much more than our words is our working out our salvation with fear and trembling that our children see. It is when you are sitting in the limo getting ready to walk into your father's funeral and your mom says to trust in the Lord and you know it is not empty words, but that she has been in this place before and knows it to be true with every fiber of her being. With that example day in and day out, when you hit your own hard you know where to turn.

Life is hard, but what we do in the hard is a choice we have to make. Will we shut down our hearts and try to numb the pain so we do not feel (risking shutting down joy as well) or will we open up our hearts to Jesus and allow Him to heal our broken hearts? He will use our brokenness to bring Him glory, allowing us to bless others in the process as we encourage them in their hard journeys.

Please pray to open your hears to the Lord's healing touch.

Scripture:

Whoever fears the Lord has a secure fortress, and for their children it will be a refuge." Proverbs 14:26

The Lord is close to those of a broken heart and saves those who are crushed in spirit. Psalm 34:18

With us is the Lord our God to help us and to fight our battles. 2 Chronicles 32:8

Be joyful in hope, patient in affliction, faithful in prayer. Romans 12:12

Sadness

I used to feel bad about feeling sad about things because I knew there are always others in situations so much worse than whatever I am going through. Now I realize that is okay to be sad. We daily have losses in life that we need to name and we need to grieve.

Our society tends to dictate what we are allowed to grieve and for how long. We need to mourn our losses so we can move on.

Author and counselor Leslie Vernick says that if you are emotionally invested in a person or thing and you suffer a loss you will be stuck because you are still emotionally invested in that person or thing unless you name it and allow yourself time to grieve the loss. Only then can you mourn and move on.

God is faithful. He meets us in our sadness. Jesus had times of sadness. We all have lots to be sad about. Pray for God to guide you to safe people you can talk to and share your sadness, people who will boldly share the hope and healing of Christ with you. Pour out your heart to the Lord allowing Him to speak truth into your loss.

Pray Psalm 139 for God to search your heart and show you any anxious thoughts. Spend some time journaling and processing what the Lord reveals. Take time to be sad, but then do not stay there. Mourn and move on. Pray that you will be willing to go there to face your grief and pain. Allow Christ to enter in to your story and find true life.

Scripture:

Blessed are those who mourn, for they will be comforted. Matthew 5:4

Grieve, mourn, and wail. James 4:9

A time to weep and a time to laugh, a time to mourn and a time to dance. Ecclesiastes 3:4

I have come that you might have life and have it abundantly John 10:10

Big Guns

Several years ago when I had a friend who had a liver disease we prayed and prayed. We had multiple prayer services. We took her to a healing service. We brought in a minister who anointed her with oil. As she got sicker one of our friends called me one day and said "Lanie I think it is time we brought out the big guns." I was like "What? What else is there?" She said, it is time we start fasting. I had four little children and was doing ministry and the thought of giving up much needed nutrition was met with much angst...at first. I prayed about it and was so convicted that I may be giving up some nutrition for a short time, but her three young children would be giving up their mom for a lifetime. We gathered our community and set up a schedule with a prayer wall and scheduled days to fast and pray. My friend passed away, but the fruit born out of the prayer and fasting in my life and the lives of the others and even in her life and her family was immense.

I had another dear friend who was a young missionary in India. She got sick and quickly her health deteriorated. She was airlifted from her village to a bigger hospital in a bigger city. A friend of the family sent out an SOS asking people to fast and pray. The end of the first day of the fasting and praying she had a miraculous turning of her condition. The doctors thought she was near death when her condition completely, miraculously turned around.

I do not begin to understand why we fast and pray and one friend lives and we fast and pray and the other friend does not. I only know that *our struggle is not against flesh and blood, but against the rulers, against the authorities, against the powers of this dark world and against the spiritual forces of evil in the heavenly realms.* Ephesians 6:12

I also know the impact that both friends' illnesses personally had on my prayer life. As I gave up food to pray specifically, I thought of how we should hunger and thirst for righteousness. It reminded me to pray. It increased the fervency of my prayers and the depth of my prayers. Food in general lost some of its hold over me. Now any time I am hungry, it reminds me of what I need to be hungry for. Instead of hunger representing a negative, it is a positive. We can fast from things other than food as well. We can fast from words, social media, and coffee. We can give up anything that is difficult to give up that will remind us to pray when we want it.

Please pray to see the benefits both now and for eternity of giving up legitimate and illegitimate things that have taken the place of God in our lives.

Scripture:

But I, when they were sick - I wore sackcloth; I afflicted myself with fasting; I prayed with head bowed on my chest. Psalm 35:13 ESV

'Yet even now,' declares the Lord, 'return to me with all your heart, with fasting, with weeping, and with mourning.' Joel 2:12

Who's Your Daddy?

Our relationship with our earthly father for better or for worse affects how we see God. If your father was strict or harsh or angry or absent you may not even realize that you perceive your heavenly father through the lens of your earthly father.

I would encourage you to take a minute and pray and write down all the characteristics of your earthly father and pray for the Lord to show you any area where those characteristics have limited how you see your heavenly Father.

If we blame the Lord for the hard things in our lives, then it inhibits our ability to run to Him with our hard things, cutting off the very source of our help. If we couldn't trust our earthly daddy, without even realizing it we have a more difficult time trusting and running to our heavenly daddy.

I have a stone in my car. It reminds me that I have a heavenly daddy that I believe desires not just to give me bread and not a stone, but cake and my favorite kind! When I start forgetting that, I put that stone in my hand and feel how solid it is and it reminds me of the solid Rock I am standing on and where my real Hope lies. It makes me think of the song "The Rock Won't Move".

> *The Rock won't move and His word is strong*
> *The Rock won't move and His love can't be undone*
> *The Rock won't move and His word is strong*
> *The Rock won't move and His love can't be undone*
> *The Rock of our Salvation.*　　Vertical Church Band

Please pray to realize that regardless of the kind of earthly daddy you have, even if you have a great one or don't have one at all, that you have a heavenly daddy who is a good, good father who will never leave you nor forsake you.

Scripture:

Ask and it will be given to you; seek and you will find; knock and the door will be opened to you. For everyone who asks receives; the one who seeks finds; and to the one who knocks, the door will be opened. Which of you, if your son asks for bread, will give him a stone? Or if he asks for a fish, will give him a snake? If you, then, though you are evil, know how to give good gifts to your children, how much more will your Father in heaven give good gifts to those who ask him! Matthew 7:7-11

Yet the Lord longs to be gracious to you; therefore He will rise up to show you compassion. Isaiah 30:18

See, I have engraved you on the palms of my hands; Isaiah 49:16

Trauma

I was surprised at the amount of trauma I felt after my wreck even though no one was injured. One part that I kept replaying in my mind was when I was walking over to the car that I hit and there was that moment when I had to make myself look in the window and see if I had hurt someone. I replayed over and over that moment and felt the fear that I might have seriously harmed someone.

I pray often that my family will not harm themselves or others, so I was greatly relieved when the lady was okay. Afterward I didn't really want to drive at all and pretty much just wanted to stay home. I got a ride the next day with a coworker and on the way to pick me up, she had a wreck. Ugh! The Lord was sweet to allow me to be snowed in that weekend.

Realizing that I was struggling with trauma after the wreck, I decided to meet with a friend to process the trauma. We talked and walked through it together and took it apart. I physically and emotionally felt better after processing it with someone else and praying together about it. I think our society underestimates the power of trauma in our lives to disable us. We go on with our lives not processing the trauma and it is exhausting to drag it around day after day. There is evidence that when we don't process our trauma it can affect our health. Society tries to tell us what qualifies, what counts as trauma. If it is traumatic to you then it is trauma. The Lord is the great physician, but we need to acknowledge areas where we need to allow Him to step in and heal and pray for Him to show us the tools we need for healing. Any place where we are stuck could be a place where there is trauma that we need to address.

Scripture:

The secret things belong to the Lord our God, but the things revealed belong to us and to our children forever, that we may follow all the words of this law. Deuteronomy 29:29

Cast all your cares upon him for He cares for you. 1 Peter 5:7

Then they cried to the Lord in their trouble, and he saved them from their distress. He brought them out of darkness, the utter darkness, and broke away their chains. Let them give thanks to the Lord for his unfailing love and his wonderful deeds for mankind, for he breaks down gates of bronze and cuts through bars of iron. Psalm 107: 13-16

Crucible Of Affliction

"It is quite easy for us to talk and to theorize about faith, but God often puts us into His crucible of affliction to test the purity of our gold and to separate the dross from the metal. How happy we are if the hurricanes that blow across life's raging sea have the effect of making Jesus more precious to us! It is better to weather the storm with Christ than to sail smooth waters without Him. J.R. Macduff" (Streams in the Desert, August 28)

I went to visit a friend who is facing a terminal illness. I have always known Jesus to be her rock. Her crucible of affliction has even more clearly defined how precious Jesus is to her. In the midst of unspeakable sadness is unspeakable joy.

I looked up the definition of crucible. 1. A vessel made of a refractory substance such as graphite or porcelain, used for melting and calcining materials at high temperatures. 2. An extremely difficult experience or situation; a severe test or trial: http://www.thefreedictionary.com

This past Sunday I went to see dear friends' son baptized. The minister shared about Kayla Mueller who was a 24 year old believer who was kidnapped and killed in captivity with ISIS. In a letter to her parents she said "By God and your prayers I have felt tenderly cradled in a free fall". Wow! That is where I am in this juncture in my life…. tenderly cradled in a free fall.

So my prayer for all of us is that we feel the Lord's tender cradle in our free fall through whatever crucible of affliction the Lord is using to teach us that he is precious and that the adversity will accomplish its complete work to remove the dross in our lives.

Scripture:

Being confident of this, that He who began a good work in you will carry it on to completion until the day of Christ Jesus. Philippians 1:6

Consider it pure joy, my brothers and sisters, whenever you face trials of many kinds, because you know that the testing of your faith produces perseverance. Let perseverance finish its work so that you may be mature and complete, not lacking anything. James 1:2-4

Stones And Shells

I love to pray with people over their homes. When friends came to do this for me, one friend brought stones that they left in each room as a reminder of the Lord's faithfulness. There was nothing magical about the stones. They were just a visual, tangible reminder of the Lord's presence in my home. That prayer walk of my home was several years ago and I still enjoy seeing those stones and even have found them in unusual places. There was one on the ground by my car as we left to take my youngest to college.

I had a friend going through a particularly difficult time and I offered to come prayer walk her house with her. I arrived and realized I had left the stones at home. I asked her if she had anything we could use and she said she had shells from their recent beach trip. As we prayed from room to room, she placed a shell somewhere in each room.

It is amazing what the Lord can do with the smallest things. Again and again my friend has told me what a blessing the shells have been. Right when she needed encouragement she would see a shell. Her daughter moved and told me that some of the shells moved with her and continue to be a reminder to her of God's faithfulness.

This friend told me recently that workmen were at her house and asked her what the deal was with the shells. The shells provided an opportunity for her to share the gospel with them. Immeasurably more than all we ask or imagine! God can take the smallest ordinary thing and perform extraordinary miracles with it.

Scripture:

And my God will meet all your needs according to the riches of His glory in Christ Jesus. Philippians 4:19

Now to Him who is able to do immeasurably more than all we ask or imagine, according to His power that is at work within us. Ephesians 3:20

Receive The Good--Let Go Of The Bad

My father loved me, but was not around for most of my life. He travelled extensively in his job and then was killed in a plane crash when I was in college. As a young adult it was difficult because there were things for which I felt I needed to forgive him, but he was not around to confront. It had me stuck in a lot of ways.

As a Young Life leader I went on a wilderness trip where we had a 30 hour solo in the woods. During that solo, I read *A Severe Mercy* by Sheldon Vanauken and had an encounter with the Lord where He showed up as my daddy. He allowed me to release to Him all my hurts from my earthly father. It was a turning point in my walk with the Lord.

Later in life, I was able to realize many gifts I had received from my father. I realized that I could embrace the good I had received from him, and at the same time I could be honest about the bad. I had to grieve that he was an absent dad and it was okay to be sad about that and grieve my losses as a result.

I think many times we feel like we have to paint a picture that it is all good and don't feel like we can be honest about the hard things. Or we move the other direction and focus only on the bad and the hard which overshadows any good that was there

It has been 34 years since I lost my earthly father. He lived life with passion and gusto. He had a huge personality and people were drawn to him. The places that he left void in my life, my heavenly daddy has filled to overflowing. The Lord has never been an absent dad, but one who provides and cares for me in every detail of my life allowing me to receive the good and let go of the bad.

Scripture:

And we know that in all things God works for the good of those who love him, who have been called according to his purpose. Romans 8:28

No, in all these things we are more than conquerors through him who loved us. Romans 8:37

How great is the love the Father has lavished on us, that we should be called children of God! And that is what we are! 1 John 3:1

Which of you, if his son asks for bread, will give him a stone? Or if he asks for a fish, will give him a snake? If you, then, though you are evil, know how to give good gifts to your children, how much more will your Father in heaven give good gifts to those who ask him! Matthew 7:9-11

Pioneers

My mom is from a family of pioneers. Her parents homesteaded in New Mexico. Her grandfather was in the run for Oklahoma.

As I understand it, if you lived on the land on which you staked a claim for a year, and paid the taxes it was yours. My great grandfather was lined up on the Oklahoma border with everyone else waiting for the gun to go off to go in and get his claim. He had a wagon and had already picked the plot of land he wanted, which was by a stream. While waiting, a man walked by on foot. Being a fine Christian man he offered to give the guy a ride in his wagon. It was late when they got to the land so they decided to bunk down for the night. The next morning he woke to the smell of breakfast. The guy was up and had made him breakfast. As he was eating the guy was telling him a story and when he was finished he told him he had just carved his initials and was claiming the land my great-grandfather had picked as his own. My great-grandfather was devastated, but went on further, found another plot and staked his claim. At the end of the year when he went to the courthouse to pay his taxes and get the deed to the land, he found out that the other land the man had taken had been zoned for a school. The man was not allowed to have it and by the time he realized it, most of the other land had already been homesteaded. What had seemed like evil and loss, had been the Lord's protection and provision.

Many times we do not get what we want. Sometimes we find out why and sometimes we do not. We just see a little. The Lord sees it all. What Satan intends for evil the Lord turns to good. I pray that when things do not go as we have planned, that we are not undone, but surrender the situation to the Lord, trusting that HIs ways are higher than ours.

Scripture:

For now we see only a reflection as in a mirror; then we shall see face to face. Now I know in part; then I shall know fully, even as I am fully known. 1 Corinthians 13:12

The secret things belong to the Lord our God, but the things revealed belong to us and to our children forever, that we may follow all the words of the law. Deuteronomy 29:29

Pray Now

Several years ago my best friend of 20 years needed a liver transplant. She got worse and worse and had finally gone to Florida to the Mayo clinic to have the transplant done. She called me the night before and said that they had seen a shadow on a former scan and were doing further testing. She asked me to pray and I said I would. She said "NO, PRAY NOW!" I said okay and prayed with her on the phone. I still remember where I was standing when we prayed. It turned out to be metastatic cancer and she came home on Mother's Day weekend with her husband to her three precious children to spend her last days with them. That was more than a decade ago, but ever since then when someone shares a need or a request I can hear my sweet friend saying "PRAY NOW!" I have since had the privilege of praying on planes, in stores, in church, on fields, on answering machines and pretty much everywhere you can imagine. I rarely get through Walmart without praying with someone.

I would encourage you to be bold. If someone shares something with you, stop right there, put your hand on their shoulder and pray for them - out loud. Your words don't have to be fancy or sound godly. If you see someone in need, offer to pray with them.

The great thing is since you learn to pray by praying – you get lots of practice. They are sharing their "pearls" with you so make sure you handle them with care. Don't share with others unless they have given you permission to do so and only the exact requests they have given.

Soon people know you are willing to pray and they start sharing requests because they believe you will actually pray and then you get to be a part of people's lives. God brings them to your mind when they need prayer and you get to hear the answers to your prayers and you get encouraged to pray more. When you wake up in the night you see it as a privilege instead of a disturbance because someone must need prayer. The more you pray, the more excited you get about praying and the more ideas God gives you of how you can pray and all of a sudden you are typing up many things that the Lord is teaching you. You get the picture!

Scripture:

And pray in the Spirit on all occasions with all kinds of prayers and requests. With this in mind, be alert and always keep on praying for all the Lord's people. Ephesians 6:18

Therefore confess your sins to each other and pray for each other so that you may be healed. The prayer of a righteous person is powerful and effective. James 5:16

One Of The Best Days Of My Life

I was a high school math teacher and then stayed home with my 4 children for many years. As my children were growing less dependent on me, I prayed that if the Lord wanted me to work that He would drop a job in my lap. I was willing, but wanted Him to clearly show me what was next.

Soon after that, I was at one of my daughter's basketball games and the friend sitting next to me offered me a job.

I just finished my 6th year in that job as an academic coach to athletes at Wake Forest University. It has been such a huge blessing in so many ways. Paula Rinehart says in her book Better Than My Dreams to find the place where the world's great needs and your gifts cross. I have found that crossroads in my job. I love to learn and I love to encourage others to love to learn. Several of the athletes that I have worked with over the past few years graduated recently. It was so special to see them accomplish this life goal and to have been a part of their journey. One thanked me and said that I always believed in him and saw something in him that he didn't see in himself.

The only eternal things in life are God and relationships. When we invest in the lives of others, speaking truth to them and cheering them along the way, we get the greatest privilege of being a part of their journey and their story. Watching them receive their diplomas made Monday one of the best days of my life.

Scripture:

As iron sharpens iron, so one person sharpens another. Proverbs 27:17

Instruct the wise and they will be wiser still; teach the righteous and they will add to their learning. Proverbs 9:9

Because we loved you so much, we were delighted to share with you not only the gospel of God but our lives as well. 1 Thessalonians 2:8

A Tool

God just wants tools.

I used to be a tool for certain people, which was actually a good boot camp for my own personal "great exchange". I exchanged being their tool for being the Lord's tool. I used to try to do both and it did not go too well.

As I compared the two it was very enlightening. I often would try so hard, but not find favor with people. But with the Lord I feel His pleasure at just the decision to be His tool.

With people, I often did not feel loved or appreciated no matter how hard I tried to please; with the Lord- oh my word – sometimes I pinch myself I feel so loved and valued and appreciated and He doesn't stop there, He lifts up real people who value me and appreciate me as well.

With certain people, I would pour out my heart and not be heard; with the Lord, I pour out my heart and feel heard and understood and even feel Him moving my heart to His. I tried and tried to do everything I was asked with the people and yet never got it right; with the Lord I don't have to work at it. I surrender to Him and it is like I am on a tube riding down the river and sometimes it is rapids and sometimes it is a pleasant stream, but I am just along for the ride not worrying what is up ahead....resting in my complete trust in Him (well... learning to rest in Him.)

With people there would be angst over the consequences of my mistakes; but with the Lord I see Him take my mistakes and use them for His glory giving me freedom to mess up.

The joys of being a tool for the Lord are limitless! *When the Lord sets us free, we are free indeed!* John 8:36. The added bonus is now I am free to be Jesus to people...loving them with His love!

Scripture:

Trust in the LORD with all your heart and lean not on your own understanding; in all your ways submit to him, and he will make your paths straight. Proverbs 3:5, 6

Many are the plans in a person's heart, but it is the Lord's purpose that prevails. Proverbs 19:21

It is better to take refuge in the LORD than to trust in humans. Psalm 118:8

But Jesus would not entrust himself to them, for he knew all people. He did not need any testimony about mankind, for he knew what was in each person. John 2:24-25

Blue Light Days

A dear friend of mine wrote the below post. She describes well how grief sneaks up and in an instant hijacks us – mind, body and soul. I think we all have blue light days, not just from grief, but it may be a comment, phone call, text, or email that completely consumes us.

I love that with two words – "blue light" we can ask others to pray without having to give a lengthy explanation. Knowing others care and are lifting us up in prayer breaks the isolation of the blue light day and encourages us to move from powerless to empowered. Before a blue light moment occurs, enlist a few others that are trustworthy who would be willing to receive your SOS and that you would in turn be willing to intercede on their behalf as well. James 5:16 *...pray for each other so that you may be healed. The prayer of a righteous person is powerful and effective.* (NIV)

Blue Light Days
Monica Rinehart Winter Saturday, October 31, 2015

Imagine you're driving in your car, when suddenly you look in the rear view mirror and see blue flashing lights.
Imagine your physical and emotional response in that moment – the panic – the anxiety – the flushed face and rise in blood pressure.
Imagine that feeling, while someone is also standing on your chest.
Imagine you have to walk around all day at work or other location with that feeling and do the things you normally have to do.

That's what it's like when grief sneaks up on you after you lose a child. It's unpredictable, instant and can consume your entire physical and emotional being, just like when you notice the blue flashing lights behind you.

I call these my "Blue Light Days". On these days, I text my sisters and a few others. They know the code. All I have to say is, "it's a blue light day" and they know to send up extra prayers.

To my family and friends who hold me up on "Blue Light Days", you are a blessing and I couldn't press on without you.

Scripture:

Therefore confess your sins to each other and pray for each other so that you may be healed. The prayer of a righteous person is powerful and effective. James 5:16

Therefore encourage one another and build each other up, just as in fact you are doing. 1 Thessalonians 5:11

Peace Plant

I gave one of my daughters a peace plant along with a peace letter. She brought the plant home last Christmas and I continue to care for it until she is ready to take it. It reminds me when I forget to water it. It wilts.

Today when I watered it, I thought about how our spirits are the same way. When we are not watered with the word of God and resting in Him and trusting Him we wilt under fear and anxiety.

Peace Letter:

For your birthday I am giving you a Peace Lily, but it is more than a plant. My prayer is that along with the plant, the Lord will bring you perfect peace. You have nothing to fear but a healthy fear of the Lord who made you and loves you completely. Rest in His love and provision for you. He will never leave you nor forsake you. He is in every detail of your life. As you surrender completely to Him and choose to obey Him, He will direct your steps, guide your path and grant you peace. Verses that have come to me as I am praying peace for you are:

Don't worry about anything, but pray and ask God for everything you need, always giving thanks for what you have. 7 And because you belong to Christ Jesus, God's peace will stand guard over all your thoughts and feelings. His peace can do this far better than our human minds. Philippians 4:6-7

For God has not given us a spirit of fear, but of power and of love and of a sound mind. 2 Timothy 1:7

You keep him in perfect peace whose mind is stayed on you, because he trusts in you. Isaiah 26:3

Peace!

Scripture:

I have told you these things, so that in me you may have peace. In this world you will have trouble. But take heart! I have overcome the world. John 16:33

Now may the Lord of peace himself give you peace at all times and in every way. The Lord be with all of you. 2 Thessalonians 3:16

Favorite Phrases

I love catch phrases and totally overuse them. I will give credit to those I heard say them first…. the ones I remember.

God is in the details. (me)

- 90% of life is showing up.
- Pray more, worry less.
- Pray BIG!
- Learn to pray by praying. (Brennan Manning)
- Pray as you can, not as you can't. (Brennan Manning)
- Don't worship created things instead of the creator. (Will Toburen)
- Obedience brings blessing, disobedience brings disaster……to the whole community. (Nancy Epperson the first part, Ken Hoglund the second)
- Purity is smart. Impurity is stupid. (Randy Alcorn, The Purity Principle)
- Pay attention to the tension. (Jane Bailey)
- The Lord leads. Satan drives. (Jane Bailey)
- Need doesn't justify a calling. (Lynn Barclay Brewer)
- Give out of your saucer, not your cup. (Lynn Barclay Brewer)
- Transform or transmit. (Jane Bailey)
- Be grateful or critical.
- No is a complete sentence. (Helen Naples)
- Don't over function. (Leslie Vernick)
- Jesus loves me. (Bible)
- Jesus loves you! (Bible)

What are yours?

Scripture:

May these words of my mouth and this meditation of my heart be pleasing in your sight, Lord, my Rock and my Redeemer. Psalm 19:14

The Spirit gives life; the flesh counts for nothing. The words I have spoken to you – they are full of the Spirit and life. John 6:63

Be Still

I have in my laundry room a sign with the verse: *The Lord will fight for you; you need only to be still.* Exodus 14:14

As I have thought about that verse, I have connected it to the verse: *Be still and know that I am God.* Psalm 46:10

Still praying about how the two work together. I think in the past, I wanted to just get in a ball and have the Lord swoop in and rescue me from difficult situations, but I am realizing that one way He is fighting for me is through teaching me to "Be still and know Him as my Lord."

A huge part of that is the "know". As I come to know Him better, over and over He proves trustworthy. Lately I realize in my conversations with Him, I will say "I would love _____, but I trust you'. The more I get to know Him, the more I see how faithful He is and that He is trustworthy. It is difficult because we know "man" and no man is trustworthy all of the time, but the Lord is. We spend so much energy pleasing others when if we focus on pleasing God we can rest in the truth that what the Lord leads will be the best for the people around us.

My prayer for you is that you will rest in the Lord and His love for you, keeping your eyes looking up into His loving gaze.

Scripture:

I keep asking that the God of our Lord Jesus Christ, the glorious Father, may give you the Spirit of wisdom and revelation, so that you may know him better. I pray that the eyes of your heart may be enlightened in order that you may know the hope to which He has called you, the riches of his glorious inheritance in His holy people and His incomparably great power for us who believe. That power is the same as the mighty strength he exerted when he raised Christ from the dead and seated him at his right hand in the heavenly realms. Ephesians 1:17-20

Stop trusting in mere humans, who have but a breath in their nostrils. Why hold them in esteem? Isaiah 2:22

Entering His Rest

Recently the Lord has been waking me up earlier than usual for my quiet times. I will feel His nudging and know I need to be obedient to get out of bed, that I need that extra time with Him. After I finish my normal quiet time routine, there has been enough time to just wallow in His great presence and love for me. It has been such a sweet time with Him. I have drawn near to Him and then have time to just rest and enjoy Him. I think most of the time in the past, I checked it off my list and moved on not realizing the benefit of just staying in that sweet spot to enjoy Him. Sometimes I fall back asleep praising Him and it is sweet sleep. Other times, I just rest in His presence.

I think it is interesting in Hebrews 4 that right after it talks about entering His rest and the ability to enter His rest when we are obedient, it goes into the power of scripture to discern our thoughts and intentions. When we spend time in HIs word and take time to enter His rest we are able to hear Him better and we allow Him into our thoughts and intentions to guide us which prevents much disobedience.

On September 3 in <u>Streams in the Desert</u>, Freda Hanbury Allen is quoted "To the still heart God does His secrets tell."

So cool how it all ties together. Right after reflecting on rest, my pastor said "Sabbath reorients your life." That perfectly connected with entering His rest and that out of that sweet time with Him we gain perspective and our lives are reoriented to His ways, which are higher than our ways. The rest of our day is less crazy because we have had time to rest in Him and re-oriented.

Scripture:

Therefore, while the promise of entering His rest still stands, let us fear lest any of you should seem to have failed to reach it.... For we who have believed enter that rest, as he has said, as I swore in my wrath, 'They shall not enter my rest.' Hebrews 4:1,3 ESV

Since therefore it remains for some to enter it, and those who formerly received the good news failed to enter because of disobedience, again he appoints a certain day, Today...Today, if you hear his voice do not harden your hearts. Hebrews 4:6-7

So then, there remains a Sabbath rest for the people of God, for whoever has entered God's rest has also rested from His works as God did from his. Let us therefore strive to enter that rest, so that no one may fall by the same sort of disobedience. For the word of God is living and active, sharper than any two-edged sword, piercing to the division of soul and spirit, of joints and of marrow, and discerning the thoughts and intentions of the heart. Hebrews 4:9-12

Final Thoughts

Emily Huck, a friend on Young Life staff said that our call starts with God and not us. In the same way our relationship with the Lord begins with Him and not us. He made us and He sacrificed Jesus in order to have a relationship with us. He is showing up in our lives every day, but the majority of the time we just are not seeing His hand at work.

Pray for eyes to see Him. Give Him the first fruits of your day even if it is a short amount of time. Give Him the last minutes of your day.

When we frame our lives with Him and surrender our hearts and minds to Him, it allows Him to move in our lives and allows Him to use us in others.

We think that doing it our way leads to freedom, but it leads to bondage. We think doing it His way leads to bondage, but it leads to freedom.

I pray that in some way these devotionals have encouraged you to walk with Him minute by minute and allow Him to freak you out every day. Thank you for taking the time to read them and I would love to hear your stories of Him showing up in your life as well--extraordinarily in your ordinary.

Scripture:

May the God of hope fill you with all joy and peace as you trust in him, so that you may overflow with hope by the power of the Holy Spirit. Romans 15:13

The grace of the Lord Jesus be with you. My love to all of you in Christ Jesus. Amen. 1 Corinthians 16:23-24

Made in the USA
Middletown, DE
15 January 2020